First Phrases from Around the World

Everyday Polish

Tricia Hoffman

Little Mitchie
an imprint of Mitchell Lane

I0799815

CREATING YOUNG NONFICTION READERS

Little Mitchie books spark curiosity and support early nonfiction reading for students in Grades 2-3. Designed to build vocabulary, support second language learners, and prepare readers for middle-grade content, each book includes helpful tips for parents and educators to build confidence and deepen understanding of the world.

TIPS FOR READING NONFICTION WITH BEGINNING READERS

Talk about Nonfiction

Begin by explaining that nonfiction books give us information that is true. The book will be organized around a specific topic or idea, and we may learn new facts through reading.

Look at the Parts

Most nonfiction books have helpful features. Our *Little Mitchie* titles include color photographs and graphic aids, a table of contents, a glossary, and an index. Share the purpose of these features with your reader.

Color Photos and Graphic Aids

A lot of information can be found by "reading" photos, charts, maps, and other graphic aids found within nonfiction texts. Help your reader learn more about the different ways information can be displayed.

Table of Contents

Located at the front of the book, this list shows the big ideas within the text and the page numbers where they can be found.

Index

Located at the back of the book, an index is an alphabetical list of topics and the page numbers where they can be found.

With a little help and guidance about reading nonfiction, you can feel good about introducing a young reader to the world of *Little Mitchie* nonfiction books.

Little Mitchie is an imprint of:

Mitchell Lane
PUBLISHERS

2001 SW 31st Avenue
Hallandale, FL 33009
mitchelllanepub.com

Copyright © 2027 by Mitchell Lane Publishers. All rights reserved. No part of this book may be reproduced without written permission from the publisher. Printed and bound in the United States of America.

First Edition, 2027.

Author: Tricia Hoffman
Designer: Kathy Walsh
Editor: Tricia Hoffman

Library of Congress Cataloging-in-Publication Data
Title: Everyday Polish / by Tricia Hoffman

Description: Hallandale, FL :
Mitchell Lane Publishers, [2027]

Identifiers:
Library bound ISBN: 979-8-89260-911-1
Paperback ISBN: 979-8-90145-062-8
eBook ISBN: 979-8-90145-021-5

Library of Congress Control Number: 2026930276

PHOTO CREDITS: Cover and Title pg: iukhym_vova, smile3377; Doodle Art: devitaayu, FourLeafLover, wanchana, veekicl, Rizky, mhatzapa, Kebon doodle, Asyam Design, piixypeach, syoko: istock: background, rica nohara; p 4, polya_olya, Pixel-Shot, fast-stock; p 5, Prostock-studio; p 6, BearFotos; p 7, KawaiiS, Eric Isselee; p 9, Tomsickova Tatyana; p 10, Bitmap Stock, Sidorov_Rusian, Zulfiska; p 11, Sergei Kolesnikov; p 12, pics five, Chiociolla, Chase D'animulls, BongoStock; p 13, Bet_Noire, PeopleImages; p 14, Khosro, comzeal images, Mariia_Malysheva; p 15, PeopleImages, Gorodenkoff; p 16, Zakharova_Elena, pics five, PeopleImages; p 17, Ljipco Smokovski; p 18, pikselstock, BearFotos, TinnaPong; p 19, BearFotos, AS photo family; p 20 Alexander_Safonov, PicMy, BearFotos; p 21, Only Fabrizio, GSDesign, Spalnic, Michael C. Gray, timltv, ZephyrMedia; p 22, Veronia Louro, Yuganov Konstantin, Ljupco Smokovski; p 23, Gorodenkoff

Table of Contents

This Is Me

Mam dziewięć lat.

I am nine years old.

Mam na imię Zofia.

My name is Zofia.

To jestem ja

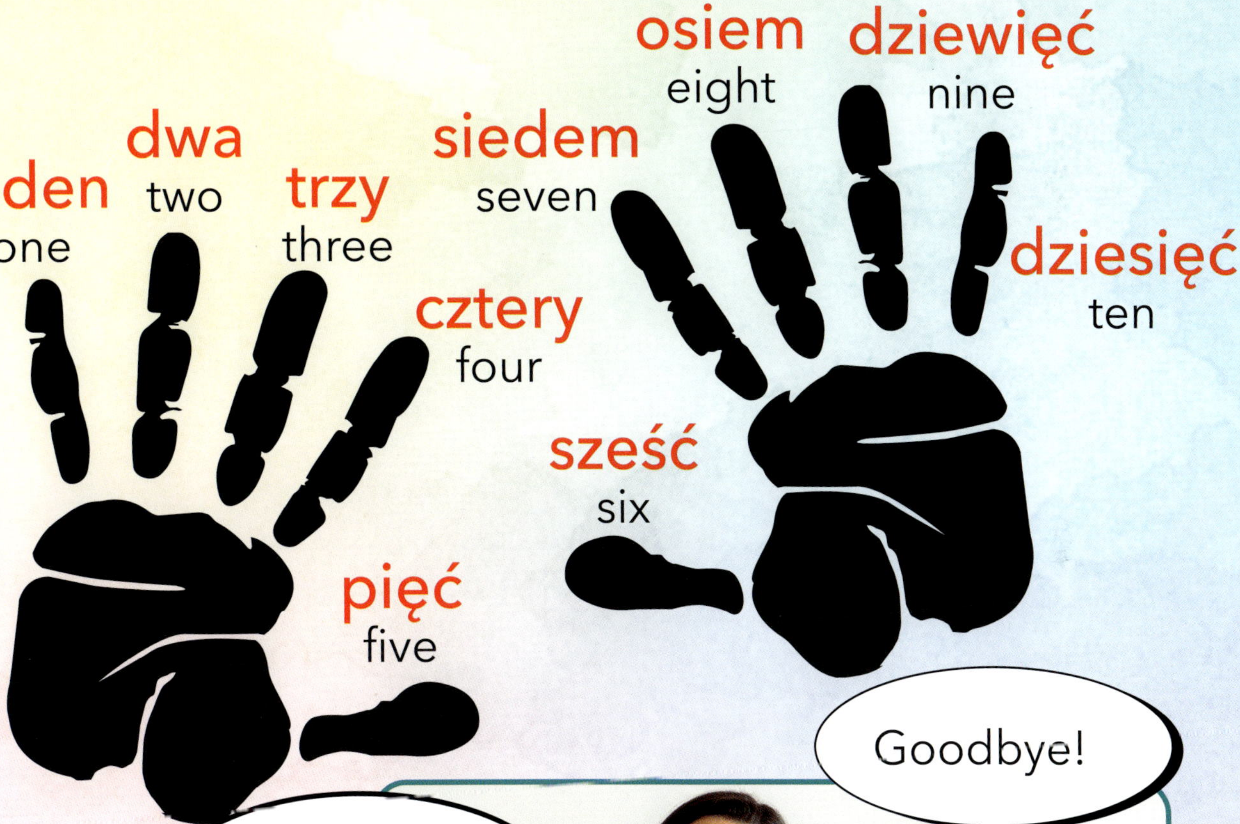
jeden
one
dwa
two
trzy
three
cztery
four
pięć
five
sześć
six
siedem
seven
osiem
eight
dziewięć
nine
dziesięć
ten

Do widzenia!
Goodbye!

People and Pets

Mieszkam z rodziną.

I live with my family.

ojciec
father

brat
brother

matka
mother

siostra
sister

Ludzie i zwierzęta domowe

Mam zwierzęta domowe.

I have pets.

pies
dog

kot
cat

ptak
bird

jaszczurka
lizard

mysz
mouse

królik
rabbit

Today

Dzisiaj jest poniedziałek.

Today is Monday.

niedziela
Sunday

poniedziałek
Monday

wtorek
Tuesday

sroda
Wednesday

czwartek
Thursday

piątek
Friday

sobota
Saturday

Jest październik.

The month is October.

styczeń . . . . . . January
luty. . . . . February
marzec . . . . . . March
kwiecień . . . . . April
maj . . . . May
czerwiec . . . . . June
lipiec . . . . July
sierpień. . . . . . August
wrzesień . . . . . September
październik. . . October
listopad. . . . . . November
grudzień . . . . . December

Dzisiaj

Na zewnątrz jest wietrznie.

It is windy outside.

słonecznie

sunny

zimno

cold

deszczowo

rainy

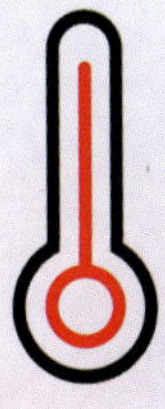

gorąco

hot

Morning

Dzień dobry!

Good morning!

Czeszę włosy.

I comb my hair.

Myję zęby.

I brush my teeth.

Poranek

Noszę zielony płaszcz.

I wear a green coat.

pomarańczowy
orange

żółty
yellow

niebieski
blue

zielony
green

fioletowy
purple

czerwony
red

różowy
pink

czarny
black

biały
white

Breakfast

Poproszę płatki na śniadanie.

I want cereal for breakfast, please.

tost
toast

sok pomarańczowy
orange juice

boczek
bacon

jajko
egg

Śniadanie

Autobus już jest.
Czas ruszać!

The bus is here.
It is time to go!

autobus szkolny
school bus

plecak
backpack

School

Chodzę do szkoły.
I go to school.

Czytam.
I read.

Uczę się matematyki.
I do math.

Szkoła

Potrzebuję pomocy.
I need help.

nauczycielka
teacher

biurko
desk

Czy mogę iść do łazienki?
May I go to the bathroom?

Time to Play

Czy pobawisz się ze mną?

Will you play with me?

Tak!

Yes!

Biegnę.
I run.

Huśtam się.
I swing.

Czas na zabawę

Neighborhood

Mieszkam w sąsiedztwie.

I live in a neighborhood.

Macham do mojego przyjaciela.

I wave to my friend.

Idę do sklepu.

I go to the store.

Sąsiedztwo

Ile to kosztuje?

How much does this cost?

sygnalizacja świetlna
traffic light

budynek
building

rower
bicycle

ulica
street

chodnik
sidewalk

Dinner

Czy to pora na kolację?

Is it time for dinner?

Tak, proszę.
Yes, please.

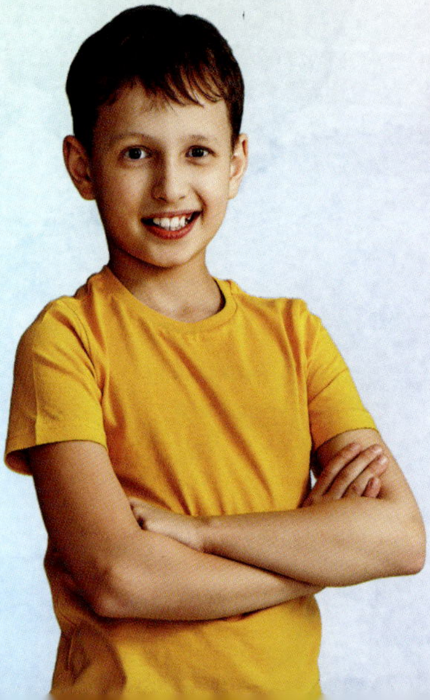

Nie, dziękuję.
No, thank you.

Kolacja

Lubię polskie jedzenie.
I like Polish food.

pierogi
dumplings

kiełbasa
sausage

gołąbki
cabbage rolls

pączki
donuts

Lubię amerykańskie jedzenie.
I like American food.

pizza
pizza

frytki
french fries

Night

Noszę piżamę.

I wear pajamas.

Idę spać.

I go to bed.

Zamykam oczy.

I close my eyes.

Noc

koc
blanket

poduszka
pillow

Index

About Polish

Polish is spoken by more than 43 million people around the world. Most Polish speakers live in Poland, where it is the official language. It is also spoken by Polish communities in other European countries such as Germany, the United Kingdom, and France. Polish is considered a challenging language to learn. It includes sounds that are not in many other languages, so pronouncing them can take practice. The Polish alphabet has 32 letters. The letters *q*, *v*, and *x* are not used in any native Polish words.